119240

THE LORD'S PRAYER

OTHER BOOKS BY OSWALD C. J. HOFFMANN

The Lord's Prayer

Oswald C. J. Hoffmann

1817

Harper & Row, Publishers, San Francisco

Cambridge, Hagerstown, New York, Philadelphia
London, Mexico City, São Paulo, Sydney

FIRST EDITION

Designer: Jim Mennick

Library of Congress Cataloging in Publication Data

Hoffmann, Oswald C. J.
  The Lord's prayer.

  1. Lord's prayer.   I. Title.
BV230.H577 1982   226'.9607   81–47834
ISBN 0–06–063999–7   AACR2

---

82 83 84 85 86 10 9 8 7 6 5 4 3 2 1

Contents

1. Conversation with the Father: Remember Me

Jesus Christ prayed. He went off by himself, if necessary, to talk to his Father. He was not secretive about it, but he did concentrate on it. When he came away from those conversations, his disciples noticed how much stronger he was.

They were impressed and probably talked about it among themselves. Maybe they even tried it and were disappointed. What happened to him did not seem to happen to them. Then they asked him, "Lord, teach us how to pray." He said, "Pray like this: 'Our Father who art in heaven.'"*

The Lord's Prayer or the "Our Father," as it has been called, is a pattern, not a formula. It is not a string of magic words. He did not pray that way himself, and he didn't want anybody else to pray that way.

---

* Biblical quotations are in the author's own translation, unless otherwise noted. Quotations from the Lord's Prayer, prolific throughout the text, are not followed by a citation of verse and Bible version quoted. The prayer can be found in Matthew 6:9–13 and Luke 11:2–4.

The Lord's Prayer does not contain any magic words, but there is power in the faith of anyone who can talk to God and call him "Father." That is something not to be despised, and God does not ignore it. It is the way the Son of God talked to his Father, knowing him and trusting him. It is the way children of God talk to God their Father today, knowing him and trusting him. As the Lord said, "This is the way: Pray like this."

We shall not spend any time arguing about the wording of the Lord's Prayer as it was originally given, or about the translation of it as we use it today. People want to know how to pray. Jesus Christ said, "Why not start out this way: 'Our Father who art in heaven'?"

The Lord's Prayer is a prayer. It is not an incantation. It is talking to God, and then listening and waiting for his reply.

The Lord's Prayer is the beginning of prayer, not the end. It is for people who want to learn how to pray. It comes from Jesus Christ himself, the Son of God and the savior of the world.

Good news needs to be told, as the apostles did when they first went out, with confidence that it is true. You don't have to be pretentious when you know something is true. You don't even have to be eloquent. St. Paul said he didn't have to worry about eloquence when he had something as powerful as the cross of Christ to talk about. In fact, eloquence can get in the way of the power of Christ's cross, which is perfectly able to take care of itself amid all of the other events of human history.

Christ is, as Martin Luther said in his great hymn, "A Mighty Fortress Is Our God," the savior of God's own sending, the savior for all people everywhere, the savior by whom the world is reconciled to God through the blood of his cross. "In him there is redemption," said Paul, "even the forgiveness of our sins" (Col. 1:14).

Praying in the name of Christ is not just a matter of form. It is praying in the confidence he gives of true forgiveness, of communion with the Spirit of the living God. Words flow in one form or another, but they always say to God, as Christ himself said, "Father."

This prayer is a starter for every kind of prayer. It tells us how to pray. Of course, prayers do not have to follow this formula. The words our Lord gave in Matthew are different from the words he gave in Luke. Obviously, he himself said the prayer in different ways. Luke's prayer is longer than the one reported by Matthew, and where Matthew says "Father in heaven," Luke says simply "Father." That's all. That's enough. That's the way faith talks, when it is faith in God, and that's the way prayer begins when it is prayer to God, the Father of our Lord Jesus Christ: "Father."

As Martin Luther said in his *Small Catechism*, when

we pray to God we should come and talk to him as children talk to their own dear fathers. The German language has two words for the single English word *you*. One term ("Du") conveys a close relationship, a familiarity; the other ("Sie") depicts a more formal, less personal meaning. When Luther translated this prayer, he used the familiar term "Du" instead of the more respectful "Sie" because that's the way fathers want their children to talk to them.

Children who love and trust their fathers do not hold them off at arms' length. We want to be close to God, trusting him and loving him, as a child loves and trusts a father.

Many people can't bring themselves to talk that way. Many of them can't bring themselves to talk to anybody that way. They are all by themselves in this wide world of ours, and they can't be close to anyone. They cannot depend on anyone else, because they have learned through bitter experience that people can depend only on themselves. It is a pitiful way to live.

I have heard husbands say about their wives, and wives about their husbands, "We never talk." You have heard children say about their parents, "There is never any conversation in our house. Nobody ever listens to me."

When husbands and wives, parents and children, have nothing to talk about, there isn't much life in the family. Whatever life there is, it is not very human. I have known people who talk more to their dogs and cats than they talk to their children. The children reciprocate by getting out of the house as quickly as they can, and as often as they can, often finding their way into all kinds of trouble—which parents then blame on the state of the world and on the spirit of rebellion that is abroad these days. Children say that parents don't care, so why should they care? Everybody blames the other fellow. It is a pitiful way to live.

In a household where members of a family talk with one another, take time to listen to one another, share joys and sorrows with one another, enlist and receive one another's help, there is something going. There is life there, and it is growing. Good communication is a sign of healthy human relationship.

The same is true for good communication with God. It is not superhuman, as some pious people would like to make it out to be. Nor is it subhuman, as it is often described by those who would make their own secular ignorance into the standard for what is good and normal and human.

Talking with God is altogether human. The Lord Jesus Christ was human, a real man. He talked with God as naturally as a person is warmed by the bright sunlight or enjoys a drink of cold, clear water. The unique and eternal Son of God was in constant communication with his Father. That's the way to be truly human, to trust in God and then stop worrying. That's the way to do it, Christ said. When you pray, start out this way: "Our Father in heaven, remember me."

The Lord's Prayer begins with God. It begins by recognizing him as Father. His strength rubs off on us. He loves us. You can believe it! The death of his Son for the sins of the world is convincing proof that he is our Father.

God is a father, not a grandfather. His children, both boys and girls, both young men and young women, both fathers and mothers, both grandfathers and grandmothers, are invited to believe in Jesus Christ and to be members of the family. God expects his sons and daughters to be worthy members of his family, living as they were meant to live. He holds them responsible for their actions, forgives what they have done wrong or failed to do right, and enlivens the future.

This is the good news of the gospel of Christ. It is for the whole world. Jesus Christ is the savior of all people everywhere. "When the time had fully come," said St. Paul, "God sent forth his son, born of woman, born under the law, to redeem those who were under the law, so that we [such as we are] might receive adoption as sons. And because you are sons, God has sent the Spirit of his Son into our hearts, crying, 'Abba! Father!'" (Gal. 4:4–6, RSV).

Anyone who prays the Lord's Prayer as Christ meant it to be prayed trusts God and believes Jesus Christ. It is as simple as that. It is also just as profound. You don't have to know everything about God to pray to him, but it is important to know him as Father, with faith in Jesus Christ that he is telling us the truth about his Father. The Spirit of his Son in the hearts of people warms them to pray, "Our Father, remember us."

Noted psychologist and writer Paul Tournier, in his *Doctor's Case Book*, tells the story of one of his patients, who was the youngest daughter in a large family. The girl was very ill, and the cost of taking care of her had added to the father's burden of supporting his large family. One day she heard him mutter in despair over her illness, "We could well have done without that one." Children can take almost anything except not being wanted by a father.

Have you ever felt that God does not want you? Is that the reason some young people rebel? Is that the reason some older people feel cynical, sullen, bitter, and hostile? Do you feel unwanted? Have you somehow gotten the idea that your sins, your failings, your shortcomings, your difference, your broken promises, the trouble you have caused, are too much for God to take? Have you left in a huff and now fear he won't take you back? Are you concerned because you don't feel at home with yourself, or you don't feel at home with God either?

Before you begin to pray, remember one thing: the great God, who has every right to pass judgment on you, loves you! The Son of God died to bring people back into the family of God. Paul said, "There is now no condemnation to those who put their confidence in Jesus Christ" (Rom. 8:1). There is no condemnation when you are forgiven by God himself. There is no condemnation when you go with Christ, believing and obeying him. There is no condemnation when you talk to God, your Father, in that family prayer of the Lord, "God, our Father in heaven, remember us, remember me."

The disciples learned to talk that way. You have to learn to talk that way. As they said, "Our Father," so do we.

Shortly after moving to a new community, a pastor went to a local barbershop for a haircut. The barber talked about many subjects, including religion. When asked if he was a member of a local church, the barber answered, "No, I'm not, but if I joined a church it would be the one down the street, the one with the steep roof."

The pastor recognized this as the church of which he had just become the shepherd. Without telling the barber who he was, the pastor asked, "Why? Why would you want to join that church?" "Well," the barber continued, "You know Dino Smith, the man who owns the store next door? That's his church, and if all the people in that church are like Dino Smith, that's where I would want to be."

I don't have to tell you what kind of a man Dino Smith is. He knows God, trusts God, and loves God. He puts his faith in Christ, and he follows Christ. Others see it in his life. When he talks to God, he says, "Our Father who art in heaven, holy be your name."

Prayer like this needs to be practiced, not just discussed. The trouble with most of us is that we discuss prayer in order to practice it. All of us need to be encouraged to pray more. In all this, we are encouraged by the Lord himself to pray like this: "Our Father who art in heaven, holy be your name among us, your kingdom come among us, and your will be done among us here on earth as it most certainly is among the hosts of heaven."

2. Our Father Who Art in Heaven

Who is up there, anyway? Is anyone up there at all? These are the questions, we are told, of the late twentieth century. Our Lord answered them in the early first century. When his disciples came to him, asking him how to pray, he told them not to heap up empty phrases as people do who want to be heard for the many words they use. "Do not be like them," Jesus said, "for your Father knows what you need before you ask him. Pray then like this: 'Our Father who art in heaven.'"

When Christ said, "our," he meant *our*. Christ did not just teach people to pray; he himself joined in. Joining in, he identified himself with all of us—our needs, our miseries, our mortal humanity.

Right where we are, amid the conflicts and confusions of life with all its fears, loneliness, and anxiety, the Lord teaches us to pray: "Our Father." With that plural, *our* Father, there goes prejudice out the door!

There go the arrogance and haughtiness that make people feel that a particular color of skin, or denominational persuasion, or national origin, or size of income, or job status, or educational achievement has given them a monopoly on God. With this "*our Father*," out the window goes all fine and fancy talk about God that would make him just like one of us, thinking and acting just as we do, interested in color of skin, or belonging to the same club, or nation, or church as we do, impressed as we are by bank accounts and titles on office doors. God has no pets, no special favorites; in other words, he is not just like everyone of us. When we make him out to be just like ourselves, we commit the supreme sin—creating God in our own image.

One of the most moving stories to come out of World War II was the sinking of the troop ship *Dorchester* off the coast of Greenland. Four chaplains— two Protestants, a Roman Catholic, and a Jew—gave their life belts to others. Holding hands on the deck, they went down with the ship.

One of these four was Rev. Clark Poling, son of the editor of the *Christian Herald*. Dr. Daniel Poling has described the turning point in the life of this young man. While attending prep school, the boy called his father long distance and told him that he had to meet him. It was very important. "I've got to see you."

The father was worried, wondering what sort of trouble his son had gotten himself into. The meeting at the train station was strained. In silence they drove to the father's office. They walked in, and Dr. Poling locked the door. Clark slumped in a chair near the desk. The father waited anxiously for the boy to begin. Suddenly Clark lifted his eyes and asked, "Dad, what do you know about God?"

His father was caught off guard. He had not expected this question. Then he began to speak. "Son, I don't know much about God, but what I know, I really know. I have tested him in joy and in sorrow, in victory and in defeat." That was the day Clark Poling set out on the path that led him into the ministry and eventually to the deck of the sinking *Dorchester*.

Who is up there, anyway? Is there anyone up there at all? Yes, there is! "Pray," Christ said, "like this: 'Our Father who art in heaven.'"

Usually, we begin with ourselves. We pray because we are desperate. Tension drives us to prayer— because of some physical illness, some unknown fear, or some sudden calamity. A terrible problem looms before us. We begin with ourselves.

Christ was not interested merely in techniques— in saying the right things at the right time in the right way. The first words of his prayer, however, show us where to begin.

Jesus tells us, first of all, to forget ourselves and to remember God. To pray, really to pray, begin with God, focusing on him, his honor, and his glory.

When you pray, begin like this: "Our Father who art in heaven."

What kind of Father is he, anyway? Many people think of him today as a feeble Father, weak and worn out, tired and tame, soft and sweet. Maybe he acted with authority once upon a time long ago, but now his muscles have become flabby. His beard grows whiter, his throne dustier, and his eyes dimmer. This old Santa Claus doesn't care much about people either. All he can do is to take care of his crotchety, creaky old self, alone and aloof from the everyday struggles of our complicated and competitive world. He is the sour, spoil-sport old man in the sky whose bark is worse than his bite—like the old man in the garden who shouts and waves his cane at the boys stealing his apples but is scarcely strong or swift enough to stop them.

The God we worship is no feeble Father. The Old Testament portrays him as young and virile, a warrior God. He is not like a crotchety old man, nor is he a killjoy crab. He is a Father whose great heart feels all the agony a human father feels when his best is not good enough for his children and they turn against him. He is a Father who wants nothing more than to be close to his children. He is a Father interested in giving only good and useful gifts to his children. He dares to give even himself. He gives for the world what is nearest and dearest to his Father's heart, his own unique and eternal Son, the apple of his eye, always obedient and never once disobedient, always understanding and always loving, always thinking of others and never of himself— him the Father gives.

When we say, "Our Father," we are saying a lot. By what right do we call him Father? Not by birth, but by rebirth. Many fuzzy ideas are going around about the Fatherhood of God and the brotherhood of man. The Fatherhood of God, like the brotherhood of man, is just talk until one really comes to know God as one's own Father.

We pray, "Our Father." By what right can you call him Father? By faith in Jesus Christ, the Son of the Father! St. Paul was not just mouthing words when he said, "You are all the children of God by faith in Jesus Christ" (Gal. 3:26). Coming to earth as a baby, living out his life without possessions, and pouring forth his lifeblood on a cross outside a city wall, the Son of God gave himself for the life of the world. And he rose from the dead. This is not just talk. It actually happened! That page can never be erased from history. It is there—his death on a Roman tree and the Easter rending of his tomb; his constant prayers for us to the Father; and his promised return to free all who trust in him from their casket prisons. Faith in Christ makes people free and keeps them God's pardoned and heaven-bound children.

Saying "Our Father," we confess ourselves to be *children* of God by faith *in Jesus Christ*. Our confidence is in that son whose life, death, and resurrection enable us to call God "Father," not as a figure of speech but in reality.

We pray, "Our Father." That's encouraging! It means that we look to him as to a loving Father, submitting our actions to his scrutiny and calling for his help to be the kind of sons and daughters he wants us to be. Like father, like son, like daughter.

We pray, "Our Father *who art in heaven*." For some, this is discouraging. If he is so far above us, as one Old Testament poet has described him, that he has to stoop way down just to see the stars; if he is way up there and I am way down here, how can he ever be concerned about me? Me—just a speck of dust on a spinning speck of dust in a universe so breathtakingly immense that it staggers the imagination?

What does this mean, that our Father is in heaven? It means that he has power to hear and to help. If he were just like you, he couldn't do much for you that you can't do for yourself. But your Father is in heaven.

He has infinite resources. Never will you come to him and say, "Will you help me?" only to have him say to you, "I would like to, but I don't have the resources." Never will you come to him and say, "I would like to know what to do," only to have him say to you, "Son, I'd like to advise you, but I just don't know what to tell you."

With the Father in command and in control, there are no accidents. He knows what he is doing. Our Father is in heaven. He is not a moody and capricious Father—not like some human fathers, on one day and off the next. God has one prevailing mood: love, for God *is* love. Even his judgments have a loving purpose behind them. In heaven we have a loving Father.

When we pray, "Our Father who art in heaven," we are not appealing to an idea way out there somewhere. Our Father is the God of the Bible, but he is not imprisoned in this book. The Bible tells the world of his mighty acts and of his great love for sons and daughters who don't act like sons and daughters— who all too frequently don't want to be his children. The Father loves. In love, he gave his Son Jesus Christ for a wayward world. In love, he reaches out to bring his wayward children back into the family and to win their affection through faith in Christ. "Like as a Father pitieth his children, so the Lord pitieth them that fear him" (Ps. 103:13, KJV).

Know him as your Father by faith in Christ. Come to him as Father by faith in Christ. By faith in Christ, pray as he told us to pray: "Our Father who art in heaven."

Who is up there anyway? Is there anyone at all? Yes, there is. The Father, of course.

The Disciples Asked the Lord: "Teach Us How to Pray."
The Lord Said, "Pray in This Way: 'Our Father Who Art in
Heaven"

Lord God, our Father in heaven, look with your grace
on us here on earth. Your Son told us to call you Father,
and so we do. We trust your Son because he died for us and
rose again. With faith in him we take our place as members
of your family, and call you Father.

Into your fatherly hands we put everything we are and
everything we have. We are yours and you are ours.

Have pity on us, our Father in heaven, and remember
that we have come by your power from the dust of the
ground, receiving from you the breath of life. Help us to
remember you in hope, receiving each day the rebirth of life
with your Spirit breathing on us forgiveness, joy, and
peace, in complete confidence that your Son died for us and
that your Son lives for us.

Lead us through the dark places and help us over the
rough spots.

Keep us from the love of things that warp our souls, and
from the evil passions that war against our souls.

Fan into flame the fire of faith within us, and warm us
with your love that we may show forth your glory in our
own humble lives, and so tell the story of your Son Jesus
with grace and power that you give to those who love you.
It is in the name of Jesus that we always pray to you, our
Father in heaven.

Amen.

3. Hallowed Be Thy Name

"Our Father who art in heaven, hallowed be thy name." With these few words, right at the outset of the Lord's Prayer, Jesus Christ took issue with every conspiracy that has ever tried to rule God out of existence, together with every culture that has ever tried to shoulder God aside as if his existence were of no importance.

I know people who would not have gotten into the last lifeboat to leave a sinking ship if someone had been in it who blatantly proclaimed faith in no God at all. I could understand feeling this way, except for the fact that some of them treat God almost as badly —making him an afterthought in their own lives, looking on him as a supplement to the real business of living, thinking about him only when they imagine they have thought everything else out for themselves, using his name to sanctify their own pride and prejudice. It is obvious from the way many good and respectable people think and act that God does not really count in their own lives; his existence or nonexistence makes no fundamental difference to them.

When God is just a useful idea to serve as a buffer against other ideas, when God does not count on the level where life is lived, his existence indeed makes no fundamental difference. Of our age, in which belief in God is commended but is regarded by many as optional, the great poet T. S. Eliot said, sadly and hauntingly, "Men have left God, not for other gods, they say, but for no God; and this has never happened before" ("Choruses from *The Rock*").

Well, it *has* happened before! That is why Christ instructed people to pray, if they are really going to pray: "Our Father who art in heaven, hallowed be thy name."

Most people do not find it easy to pray. Days and weeks pass by with no word spoken to God. We know we should pray; at times we want to pray, but little or nothing comes forth. The mind is dull and the spirit sluggish.

Has this happened to you? You begin to pray, and your mind runs dry? When you look at yourself, are you reminded of a deserted little chapel in a ghost town in the western part of the United States? Flowing sand covers the altar; the candles no longer burn; not a sound is heard. Has your mind been deserted in the same fashion? Your thoughts don't flow, and finally you give up the futile attempt? Another prayer is stillborn.

Our Lord teaches us how to pray. The first gesture

has to be a hand reached out to God, as to a Father. The hand is not a fist; it is open, ready to receive. In the hand is this petition, "Hallowed be thy name."

What's in a name, anyway? In the Old Testament, the name of God—indeed the very letters of the name of God—were considered so sacred that a person would not dare even to pronounce them. Jesus Christ had no such formalism.

Names used to mean much more than they do today. There was a time when Miller was the miller; Taylor was the tailor; Smith was the smith; Johnson was John's son; and it could very well be that the original Longfellow was a long fellow. "Tiny," "Slim," "Red" or "Curly" are common nicknames for people who may or may not resemble the name.

The name of God describes him as he is. That one name, "Father," includes everything one needs to know about God. The majesty of his creation, his love constantly rescuing his people, his steadfast love and faithfulness sending a savior to rescue a world from its waywardness and sin, his readiness to meet his people in the power of his living word— all this is in the prayer our Lord has given us to pray: "Our Father who art in heaven, hallowed be thy name."

The very first time the name of God appears in the holy scriptures, it conveys a sense of strength and power. With all the might and rule at his command, the great God wrests the world from its primeval chaos, and with a word molds all that is in heaven and earth. Of him the church has said since apostolic days, "I believe in God the *Father almighty*, maker of heaven and earth." Almighty he is, and maker of heaven and earth—yet always Father.

What do we pray for when we say, "Hallowed be thy name"? We pray that the great God, the almighty, the most high, may be recognized and known throughout the world—and indeed among us who pray—for what he is: almighty and loving Father, mighty, holy, eternal God, approachable as a loving Father by his loving children.

Christ knew his Father—who he is, what he is like, and how he feels toward the world he has made. Christ knew his Father—that he does not impose himself on his wayward children except to restrain them from destroying themselves and the world he has made; that he will stop at nothing in order to win them back from their waywardness that takes them farther away from his fatherly heart. For this Christ himself came, sent by his Father, to be a shepherd giving his life for the sheep; to be the door through which faithful people go in and out and find pasture; to be the bread and water of life, that people may eat and drink and never hunger or thirst again; to be the suffering savior and the victor over sin and death. Whoever has seen Christ has seen the Father.

Whoever knows Christ knows the Father. In Christ, the name of the Father has been hallowed for all the world to see and to know. In Christ, we pray, "Our Father who art in heaven, hallowed be thy name."

Christ was a dutiful Son to his heavenly Father. For us who are often negligent and disobedient, he was steadfastly obedient. For us who frequently push God aside and treat him as an afterthought, the Son of God always did the will of his Father and glorified his holy name. For us who grouse and grumble when we ought to pray and praise his holy name, Christ went to his cross and was given a name that is above every name, that at the name of Jesus every knee should bow, of things in heaven and earth and things under the earth, and every tongue confess that he is Lord. What do we pray for? We pray for that faith in Christ, that warm love of Christ, that Christ-like readiness to obey, that Christly spirit of forgiveness and healing and strength and courage by which the name of our Father in heaven is hallowed. For this we pray, "Hallowed be thy name."

The first thought of true prayer is the Father, and its first attitude is reverence, adoration, and thanksgiving. First come the Father and his holy name. Here there is no "give me this or give me that." That has its place—it comes later. In a world where people always put themselves first, where self-gratification is regarded as the greatest good, people must learn what really comes first: "Hallowed be thy name."

This one little petition rules out all those popular and petty little religiosities by which people hope to sell themselves to God—or to anyone who will pay them the least bit of attention. There goes all that religious and nonreligious righteousness that feeds on pride and nurtures prejudice. There goes every form of discrimination, based on any kind of difference whatever that may exist among people today. There go all those moral detours and all that disrespect for God that appears in so many private conversations: "Our Father who art in heaven, hallowed be thy name."

One thing might be added: there goes that prevalent habit of dragging the name of God in the dirt, even if only in the disrespect of vulgar profanity—the kind of thing that has caused people of the English-speaking world to be known among primitive tribes as "God-damns" because this expression happened to pop up in almost every sentence of the people these simple folk first came to know. The name of God can be a household word without being thrown into the garbage can. His name is a household word among those who pray, "Father, hallowed be thy name."

In this prayer, Christ is more interested in what we are than in what we do. What kind of a person are you anyway? What is important to you? If you live for money, furniture, automobiles, clothes, parties, and fun—just for that and nothing more—then you know what you are and you tell the whole world what you are. If *things* mean everything to you, you are going the way of those *things*.

The things that distract us from our Father are real. But so is the new life in Christ, that great and real life in which people become what God intends them to be through faith in the living Lord of life and of death, to which Christ would lead all of us with this prayer, "Hallowed be thy name." Faith in Christ and in the name of the Father are all-important. The name of the Father is written all over people who trust in Christ. They pray—really pray and really mean it—"Our Father who art in heaven, hallowed be thy name." Pray it, my friend, and mean it.

The Disciples Asked the Lord, "Teach Us How to Pray." The Lord Said, "Pray in This Way: 'Hallowed Be Thy Name'"

Our Father in heaven, your name will always be holy whether we recognize it as holy or not. We pray that your name will be holy among us, too.

Your holy name, which represents everything you are and everything you do, gave us your son Jesus to be our savior. In your holy name he came, and in your holy name he died. In your great and holy name he was raised from the dead and declared to be the Son of God, with power. We bow before the name of Jesus; his name to us is your holy name.

We give you thanks for your holy name in the gospel of Jesus the messiah. We give our hearts to you and ask you to mold them, with the grace and glory of your holy name.

We are not much, but you are everything. We pray you to let your name be holy among us as we serve and worship you. If it be your will, let those who do not know you come to know your holy name through us. Put your holy name on the banners of our lives. Give us great good spirit to hold high the banner of the cross of your Son Jesus, and write your holy name there for people to see, that they may know you, trust you, and follow you, our Father in heaven. In this, as in all our prayers, we come to you in the name of Jesus the messiah.

Amen.

4. Thy Kingdom Come

"Our Father who art in heaven, thy kingdom come."

I have heard it said that people 2,000 years ago understood all this talk about the kingdom much better than we do today. After our Lord's resurrection and just before his ascension, the men who were closest to him were still asking, "Lord, is this the time when you are going to restore the kingdom to Israel?" (Acts 1:6). The question drew from him no wry comment or, as it might have earlier, a reply in the form of a parable. The time was growing short and he had something to say: "It is not for you to know the times or the seasons, which the Father hath put in his own *power*. But ye shall receive *power*, after that the Holy Ghost is come upon you: and ye shall be witnesses unto me both in Jerusalem, and in all Judea, and in Samaria, and unto the uttermost part of the earth" (Acts 1:7–8, KJV). Ten days later, these few men knew, better than anyone could have told them, what all must pray for when they say, "Our Father who art in heaven, thy kingdom come."

We can know what it means today, and we can pray it today. Today, on college campuses and in airline terminals, at lunch counters and cocktail parties, people talk and act as if God has gone away somewhere. Some are so bold as to claim that they have done away with him. One English bishop, John A. Robinson, shaken by what people are saying and doing, wrote a book picturing God in a quite unbiblical way in order to help people, so he thought, honestly face up to the fact that God is very real. His book *Honest to God* was a best-seller. It brought forth a rash of replies with dramatic titles like *For Christ's Sake*, analyzing and trying to answer the same questions.

Our Lord never spent time trying to prove to people that God is. Apparently, he felt that nothing can be done to prevent someone from playing the fool if he or she insists on talking and acting as if God doesn't exist.

Christ knew that God is. He called him Father. Christ knew how the Father feels toward the world he has made; how disappointed in people, the crown of his creation; how ready to do all to repair the damage done by human willfulness and sin; how swift to pass judgment on sin of every kind; how generous, patient, and long-suffering toward sinners, however bitter and hostile they might be against him. Christ knew that out of love for sinful humanity he formulated the plan to redeem the world and then carried it out; that he sent his only Son, dutiful and obedient, to be a sacrifice for sin and the savior of all men; that all of this worked out from time immemorial to the moment when Christ was speaking. Knowing all this, Christ instructed his followers to pray, "Thy kingdom come!"

There are few kings today, and fewer kingdoms. If we were going to translate this petition into completely understandable terms for today, we would probably have to say, "Let God show himself to be boss." Or, in biblical terms, "Let God be king of kings and lord of lords" in the hearts of all who pray, and in the whole wide world, "Thy kingdom come!"

The odds seem to be against God, against the coming of his kingdom. Some people don't—or won't—believe. They don't believe in a personal God, and they don't believe there is a personal devil. The failure or refusal of these people to accept the personality of good or evil is probably the first good clue to the fact that there *is* a devil. The Bible gives a pretty good biography of him, and the history of the world is full of illustrations of his work. Yet some people still talk about the forces of evil at work in the world as if they were completely impersonal, dispassionate, and without any purpose to drag people away from God.

The personal forces working against God in the world have impersonal allies. One is the world itself. Please, do not misunderstand. I do not think that the world is all bad or that "touch not, taste not, and handle not" applies to everything in the world. God made this world of ours, and built into it a great deal of plain, ordinary, old-fashioned happiness. God smiles when his children have a good time. Otherwise, there would not be so much beauty in the world.

There are forces at work in the world, however, to spoil the pleasure of God and of his children. Some people don't know how to enjoy God's good gifts. They are never satisfied. "Greed" is often their middle name. They will try any kind of trick to get more for themselves, even if it means pain for someone else. Wherever people turn away from God, it has always been that way, and it is that way today. That is why there are wars between nations, conflicts between classes, and strife among people.

People not only have lost the faculty of enjoying God's good gifts; they actually use them in the wrong way. In every one of us there is a fat streak of body lust for pleasure God has forbidden. Don't kid yourself about this; you are no exception. Someone has called this a streak of slobbery, leading us to turn so many good things into wrong channels. There is something inside each one of us that makes it difficult for God's kingdom to come, for God's rule to take hold among us.

Added to all the rest, there are organized movements in the world dedicated to the proposition that God's kingdom is not real, having nothing to do with real life in our real world. "We've got to take matters into our own hands," these people tell us, "to make sure things turn out right for ourselves and our loved ones." Self-reliance, in itself, is not a bad thing; it becomes bad only when God is left out of the picture completely. Leave God out, and self-reliance produces a cesspool of bad planning with unending eyesores of unhappiness, disappointment, and grief.

I have actually heard people talk about building God's kingdom. As if any of us could do that! "His kingdom comes," as Martin Luther said, "indeed without our prayers. We pray in this petition, however, that it may come among us also."

"Thy kingdom come!" In this prayer, we quit playing bingo with life, hoping against hope that someday we shall hit the jackpot. We quit pinning our hopes to the private wheel of fortune, which spins round and round but always seems stacked against us. We put ourselves on the side of God, where everyone must be who wishes to enjoy life to the full. "Thy kingdom come!"

People may call this sanctified foolishness, but Christ knew it made a lot of sense. He prayed boldly himself. He expects us to pray in the same way: "Thy kingdom come."

When we pray, as Christ taught us to pray, we say three things at the same time: "Thy kingdom came!

Thy kingdom is coming! Thy kingdom will come!"

His kingdom has come. On this settled fact, the confidence of prayer is built. The kingdom of God has been coming ever since God first said, "Let us make man" (Gen. 1:26, RSV). The kingdom of God came in the mighty acts of the past, where God showed his hand in a marvelous way. In a unique way, for which there was no precedent in the history of the world, God sent his Son to be a human being. His life, death, and resurrection are the antecedent for everything that has happened since that time. This did not happen in a vacuum or in a corner somewhere. It is out there on the pages of history for everybody to see.

You see it all in Christ, who gave us this prayer. He lived for all of us, he died for all of us, and he rose for all of us. In him there is forgiveness, and to him all faith must be directed for this life as well as for the life to come. It is all summarized in his own words, "The time is fulfilled; the kingdom of God is at hand; repent and believe the gospel" (Mark 1:15). Speaking of himself, his power, his truth, his grace, our Lord said, "The kingdom of God has come to you" (Luke 17:21).

When God acts, people had better pay attention. In Christ, God acted. With Christ, the kingdom or rule of God came in a special way. In Christ, the kingdom of God comes to people today. Old barriers are disappearing and faith is coming into its own: complete, confident, trusting faith in the God who lets his kingdom come.

Let there be no misunderstanding about this. Jesus Christ did everything necessary to make the kingdom of God come. He needed no help of any kind. The kingdom needs no help today. All of Christ's friends fled at the time of his crucifixion. Even if all of us should flee today, the kingdom still comes.

The kingdom is God's gift, an inheritance prepared for those who love God. It can't be earned, and no one is in a position to deserve it. God gives it completely and freely. For this people are baptized in the name of the triune God. For this they grow in the knowledge and in the grace of our Lord Jesus Christ. For this they give themselves in willing service. To this they look forward for complete fulfillment. The time and place they leave completely up to God. This is the way to live! For this we pray, "Thy kingdom come."

Here is a woman who thought she was doing all right in this world. She was a good woman, a nominal member of the church, successful in business, and rearing a fine family. She took her faith for granted much as people take their citizenship for granted. She paid her taxes and took care of her obligations to the church in much the same way. In a moment of great crisis, she discovered what had passed her by; she saw Christ as he really is, the crucified and risen Lord of life. From that moment on, she was a changed woman. Still a good woman, she found a new purpose in life. She found a new sense of direction just at a time when many people lose theirs: in times of difficulty or disaster. A sense of direction is what we pray for when we say, "Thy kingdom come!"

This petition has a built-in invitation to enjoy that righteousness, joy, and peace that are the gift of the Spirit of God. The kingdom of God has come, the kingdom of God is coming, and the kingdom of God will come. For the kingdom still to come, we pray, "Father, let thy kingdom come!"

As surely as this day has dawned, God's kingdom will come. You can turn off these words if they jar you, but you can't stop God's kingdom from coming. The final fulfillment of God's kingdom could break in on the world before you have finished breakfast tomorrow morning. It is a sobering thought: Are you ready to greet the king of kings and the lord of lords?

I pray that you will know him now for what he is and what he claims to be, the Son of God and the savior of the world. I pray with all my heart that his Spirit will move your heart this day, so that when we gather at the banquet table of the king, your face will be there, radiating that righteousness, joy, and peace that the Spirit of God gives to all—and I do mean *all*—who put their trust in Christ. For this I pray personally: "Our Father who art in heaven, let thy kingdom come!"

You can pray it too.

The Disciples Asked the Lord: "Teach Us How to Pray." The Lord Said, "Pray in This Way: 'Thy Kingdom Come'"

Dear Father in heaven, your kingdom is coming all the time even though we do not pray for it. We pray that it may come among us, too. It is your kingdom, Lord God Almighty.

You rule over all. Make us the people of your pasture and the sheep of your hand.

Send into our hearts the good news of your salvation in Jesus Christ, your Son and our savior.

Forgive our sins and give us the life that is life indeed.

Help us to live as citizens of your kingdom, recognizing you as king and ourselves as children of the kingdom. By your grace and power, make us children in your family and worthy citizens of your kingdom.

Yours is the kingdom forever and ever, our Father in heaven. We pray to you as always in the great and saving name of your Son Jesus, the prince of life and the proclaimer of the kingdom.

Amen.

5. Thy Will Be Done

"Our Father who art in heaven, thy will be done on earth as it is in heaven."

In his book *Dreams of an Astronomer*, Camile Flammarion describes an imaginary trip to Mars (35 million miles away), and then to Neptune (2 billion, 700 million miles away), and then to the nearest star, Alpha Centauri (23½ trillion miles away). Proceeding from this point into outer space, the author describes earth as a little, second-rate planet, related to a second-rate sun, existing in space like a tiny room in a solar mansion. Although we cannot yet study those vast distances, the days of close-up electronic observation of our solar system are here.

People call this the scientific age. It is a remarkable fact, of course, that millions of people in this age are trying to read their future in horoscopes printed in some almanac or by the daily newspaper. Looked at critically, the scientific age is not one so much of disbelief in God as of belief in all kinds of gods.

It is nothing short of astonishing that belief in the living God should appear suspect in a scientific age while other faiths with no rational basis whatsoever,

demanding blind acceptance on the part of their ad-
herents, find ready obedience. The problem of our
age is not that people believe nothing at all, but that
they will believe almost anything at all. So it happens that a hopeless idealism, like the philosophy of
Marxism, holds an appeal for people in various parts
of the world, while the intelligent person in Russia,
so I am told, has seen the whole business tried and
found wanting, has already given up on it, and is
looking around for something else to satisfy his or
her deepest needs.

It is for an age like this, as well as for the one in
which he lived and worked, that our Lord gave this
prayer: "Our Father who art in heaven, thy will be
done on earth as it is in heaven." Cutting through all
the mystic haze created by a senseless and insatiable
appetite for believing the wrong things, Christ spoke
truth. We feel it in our bones to be true: There is
God, the Father almighty, maker of heaven and
earth. What he wills, no matter what, will be. His
will must be done on Earth as it is in heaven. We
pray in this petition that it may be done among us
also: "Father, thy will be done on earth as it is in
heaven."

Behind this prayer is a conviction—an absolute
assurance—that the will of God is good and gracious. Christ knew God as his Father. Knowing his
Father, he knew the will of God to be worth the

prayer. Knowing the will of God, he instructed all of his followers to pray in this way: "Father, thy will be done on earth as it is in heaven."

How is it with you? Do you think it is worth praying that the will of God be done for you? How seriously do you take God's will? Do you daily remember that the will of God touches all you are and everything you do?

Does God really know about those new hopes that have not yet come true or about the old ones that did not turn out at all? About the new job or the dream of becoming an artist or an engineer? About that automobile accident, or about cancer, or about the test to be given next week?

Does God really care about the world he has made and, apparently, set adrift to go it on its own? Has he ever thought about starvation and frustration, the population explosion and automation? Does he care about you, your pains or your prejudice, your anxieties and the image you would like other people to have of you, your feuds and your fears? Yes, he does care! The prayer is worthwhile: "Thy will be done on earth as it is in heaven."

Despite all the marvelous discoveries of this modern age, which should have led us in another direction, many people have fallen back on the mechanical and mistaken idea that God's will is something like the wind of fate. They imagine God is just a rubber

stamp and that his will is like a great grinder cutting
up everything in its path—or like a monstrous
steamroller lumbering across the pages of history, all
unknowing, smashing unknown people who happen to get in its way. If that is the will of God, there
is only one way to deal with it: throw in the towel
and give up. What will be, will be!

All this fatalistic thinking is a massive coverup for
our basic unwillingness, quite typical of the twentieth century, to acknowledge the existence of a personal God who deals with people in the only way
people can be dealt with—actively and personally.
To avoid that acknowledgment, we poor moderns
have to ignore or even rewrite our history. Right
within our own history, God has shown what he is
like and what he will do.

Bible history is real history, and it is reliable. At the
same time, it is more than history; it is the story of
God's will in action. When God wants to do something, he goes ahead and does it. When God wants to
correct a situation, he proceeds to do something
about it. From what he has done in human history,
one fact becomes evident: whatever he does or wants
to do is *good*. He always has a gracious purpose. He
wants to benefit the world, not destroy it. He doesn't
want anyone to perish, but that all should be saved
and come to the knowledge of the truth. That is the
way he is, and that is his will. For this we pray in this

petition, that his will may be done: "Father, thy will be done on earth as it is in heaven."

Everything that happens in accord with God's will is good. Whenever anything happens contrary to his will, it is not good. That is why we pray that his will may be done on earth. Heaven is where God's will is done with no questions asked. Earth is not heaven. Here there are people who ask questions, have doubts, disbelieve, rebel, and definitely turn to their own way. That is why Christ told us to pray: "Father, *thy* will be done on earth as it is in heaven."

God's good and gracious will is going to be done. From our point of view, it is really a wonder that God should any longer be interested, when the selfish greed and hate of people and nations seem about to inundate the whole world. God, however, does not give up. He is faithful to his purpose, always good and gracious. His word is still effective. The word that created the world, the word that redeemed the world, still comes to us to rescue and to give life. This is the greatness of a gracious God that makes people say even today, "How great thou art!"

The great God does not force his intentions on us. Having given us a free choice, he will not take back what he has given. The strategic blow has been dealt. Christ has come. Christ has defeated sin and death. Evil has been robbed of its power. Mopping-up operations still continue, until all wrongs shall be righted and all tears shall be dried. Even at this moment, however, Christ reigns, if not in the hearts of all people, at least in the magnitude of his power over all. God's will is going to be done.

What can this mean for you? The goodwill of God comes to you even now in Jesus Christ. The Father sent his Son to be the savior of the world, and he is your savior. Why not trust him? The Son of God lived and died for you. In him there is forgiveness for every sin, every willful act taking you away from God. Why not accept his forgiveness? It is yours for the taking.

God's good and gracious will calls for acceptance. God can't be manipulated and he will not hold still for all kinds of fancy maneuvers. He has to be taken as he is. Put yourself in line for his goodness. Accept his gracious forgiveness and offer your forgiven self to him in this prayer, both personal and universal: "Father, thy will be done on earth as it is in heaven."

God's will offers a place of dignity for you in the unfolding of his blueprint for the world. He knows and he cares. He knows you and he cares for you. You can depend on it. His will is powerfully at work in the world. The only question is whether you are going to be part of his purpose, an instrument to bring cheer to the lonely, aid to the physically and spiritually distressed, and a blessing to all who live around you.

The temptation is strong to ignore God's will. God's will calls for action; most of us have a strong yen for inertia. It's all right to think of God's will being done in distant heaven, but here on earth? That's another matter! It is much more comfortable to keep God's will where it belongs, up there in heaven. It is uncomfortable to face the fact that God's will has to do with living. It is done right here on earth.

When we pray, "Thy will be done on earth as it is in heaven," we are asking for it. As someone has pointed out, this is a perilous prayer. Pray at your own risk! When you pray, "Thy will be done," you lay your life on the dotted line saying, "Here am I, send me" (Isa. 6:8b, KJV).

Why does God tell us to pray this way? Because our own will is so often set against God's will. The battle against evil is all around us, but we prefer not to take part. What's the use, we ask? "Evil will win out anyway," we think. So it would appear sometimes until we remember that God's will is going to be done, no matter what. That being true, the question is squarely up to you: are you going to pray or not? Pray, remembering what you are doing. Commit yourself once and for all: "Thy will be done on earth as it is in heaven!"

Pray in the full confidence that God's will is going to be done. Be a true child of God by faith in Jesus

Christ. Faith in Christ works. It does not fail. God does watch out for his own. He knows and he cares. Pray for what is not only possible but certain: "Thy will be done on earth as it is in heaven."

After all, God is your Father. Your Father sent his Son to die for you. Your Father gives you salvation, firm and sure, through faith in Christ. Your Father took weak and retiring people, making them prophets and apostles, disciples and witnesses, that there might be children willing to use their lives to do the will of God in our own time. Your Father did and does all of this for you.

The Father's will is going to be done. His will guarantees that, following him by faith, you will be on the right path. Whatever decisions you make will be the right decisions. If they are not right in themselves—because none of us has the insight or the foresight of God—he will make them right in his own way. Don't just stand there then, asking, "What is God's will for me?" Pray, "Father who art in heaven, thy will be done on earth as it is in heaven.... Thy will be done in me."

The Disciples Asked the Lord: "Teach Us How to Pray."
The Lord Said, "Pray in This Way: 'Thy Will Be Done on Earth as It Is in Heaven'"

Our Father in heaven, we know your will toward us is gracious and good. We have that good word from your Son Jesus, and we believe him.

Your will is more important than ours, your way better for the world than ours. Let your will be done on earth as it is in heaven.

In the good news of your Son Jesus, let your will be made known to all the earth. Send your Spirit into the hearts of people that they may believe in your Son Jesus, and so fulfill your will. Help us to believe in your Son, Jesus, that we may fulfill your will.

It is your will that none should perish but all turn to you and be saved. Let your will be done on earth as it is in heaven, our Father in heaven.

Amen.

6. Give Us This Day Our Daily Bread

"Our Father who art in heaven, give us this day our daily bread."

Someone has called this the *easy* prayer. "Now we know what you are talking about," people say, "when you pray for bread." An empty stomach is a pretty obvious reminder of a fundamental need of all people.

But the prayer is not as easy as it looks. It takes faith to pray, "Give us this day our daily bread."

People don't feel it is necessary to pray just because people get hungry two or three times a day, and bread is the most natural and basic answer to that need in many parts of the world. Bread will come anyway, won't it?

Many people find it difficult to pray to God for bread. If they recognize God at all, occasionally in times of great stress, they fail to see in him the giver of ordinary things like daily bread. Why pray to God for something we get for ourselves?

Still others regard bread, or its equivalent, as our

only real need. In spite of everything Christ said, they insist that we do, indeed, live by bread alone. In their number are materialists of every description in every country of the world. If bread means everything, they ask, why not *begin* the prayer with this petition: "Give us this day our daily bread"? Of course, they are not about to pray to God for anything at all, because who needs to pray for what the good earth brings forth all on its own?

The Lord's Prayer tells us something about earth and the world in which we live. We are all strangers on earth and in this whole universe if we have never learned to pray, "Our Father who art in heaven, hallowed be thy name. Thy kingdom come. Thy will be done on earth as it is in heaven." Furthermore, we are altogether mistaken if we think that is the end of it—that our regular daily needs of body as well as of soul are beyond the care and concern of God.

The first request of our Lord's Prayer, following reverence of the person of God, praise of the name of God, and recognition of his will and purpose in the world, is for bread! We pray for our bodies. Without apology, we pray for what will meet the needs of the body, that wonderful body God himself has given each of us. After that, we proceed to the mental and spiritual needs everyone has.

This is the way our Lord wanted it. He knew people. He started with our very existence. We must be kept alive. When we pray, we ought to ask for all that will sustain our bodies and lives. We are not to spiritualize our existence as if there were nothing physical about it. If we attempt to spiritualize the body out of existence, as some philosophers (both ancient and modern) have tried to do, we misrepresent life. In fact, we do not understand it at all. Our Lord understood. He told us to pray, "Give us this day our daily bread."

What is meant by "daily bread"? Let's not waste time looking for some deep spiritual meaning hidden somewhere in this ordinary expression. It means *food*.

A friend of mine from Great Britain was captured in the early days of World War II and spent five years in a German prison camp. The main fare of these prisoners was bread, plain but filling dark bread. Every group of eight prisoners was given a loaf of bread at the beginning of each day. This particular group of prisoners had a string with eight notches in it to help them cut that loaf into eight fairly equal pieces. Each day another prisoner got his chance to cut the loaf. My friend tells me that he can still remember the good feeling that came over him every eighth day when it was his turn to cut the loaf, because the man who cut the loaf had his first choice of the pieces that he had cut.

At the seminary he had attended, this man had

been taught that the "daily bread" of the Lord's Prayer had to do with some kind of spiritual loaf, possibly related to the bread of life referred to in John (Chap. 6). In the prison camp, however, he discovered what the prayer really means. It means bread: everyday, down-to-earth bread, the kind people need in order to live. Here he learned, too, what it means to pray, "Give us this day our daily bread."

Martin Luther put it this way: "Here we consider the poor bread basket, the needs of our body and our life on earth. This petition includes everything that belongs to our entire life in this world; only for its sake do we need daily bread." Luther also suggested that instead of putting a wreath or a lion on their coats of arms, the leaders and governments of this world would be better advised to put a loaf of bread there. Related to daily bread are all the needs and wants of the body and of life on earth. Luther did not hesitate to enumerate some of them: "Daily bread includes everything needed for this life, such as food and clothing, home and property, work and income, a devoted family, an orderly community, good government, favorable weather, peace and health, a good name, and true friends and neighbors" (*Small Catechism*).

God supplies the needs of life here on earth, fulfilling his own purpose in creating us. God intends to preserve us—we are created in the divine image and do not attain our purpose in life until we are in fellowship with God, our creator.

Every year someone tries to figure out what the chemicals making up the human body are worth. It serves little purpose. No price can be set on our bodies and lives. All of us feel that the Psalmist knew what he was talking about when he said a long time ago: "Lord, how merciful are thy works! In wisdom hast thou made them all; the earth is full of thy creatures. . . . These all look to thee, to give them their food in due season. When thou givest to them, they gather it up; when thou openest thy hand, they are filled with good things" (Psalm 104:24, 27, 28, RSV).

The whole 104th Psalm talks about the stuff of which life is made. God is the giver of the raw materials of the earth. He is the giver of the products of the field, the vineyard and the orchard, the hills and the plains, together with the strength, skill, and ingenuity to produce food and to build industry for our enrichment and enjoyment. To label God's gifts as unimportant, or even sinful, is possible only when we have forgotten that God created life and that he sustains it by his almighty word. He gives "daily bread."

Our Lord's Prayer tells us how the daily bread God gives should be received—with the open hand of thanksgiving. It is to be received, not worshipped. Some people live to eat, rather than eating to live. Some live only for homes, food, appliances, and automobiles, forgetting what life is really all about. They get so absorbed in work, parties, money, and pleasure that they forget what it means to live. Some treat government, family, and friends simply as devices to secure power without any thought of helping to build an orderly and peaceable community, abusing God's good gifts for their own benefit instead of using them for his glory. Many simply don't pray, "Give us this day our daily bread."

What these people really want, apparently, is the gift without the giver, who not only wants us all to be saved and to be warm-hearted members of his family, but who also wants us all to have bread to eat and to receive that bread with thanksgiving.

Our Lord told a haunting story about a man for whom bread was everything. He tore down his barns and built bigger ones to store his possessions; then he said to himself: "Soul, you have ample goods laid up for many years; take your ease, eat, drink, and be merry. But God said to him, "Fool! This night your soul is required of you; and the things you have prepared, whose will they be?" (Luke 12:19–20, RSV). In this world where God has set up the rules, nobody will find security trying to live by bread alone.

A poll was conducted to see what people regard as their greatest worry. Forty-five percent of those interviewed said what they worried about most was money. But God did not make us in order to produce millions of worriers. I am not here to tell you not to worry, but I *can* tell you where to put your worries: give them to God and let him do the worrying!

To do this, of course, you have to know God. You won't do it unless you know him as our Lord Jesus knew him. Christ knew God as his Father. Knowing his Father, he taught us to pray, "Father who art in heaven, give us this day our daily bread."

People need bread, or rice, or meat and potatoes, or whatever it is they eat to keep alive. However, we simply can't live by bread alone. We cannot live by ourselves alone. We need the giver, and we need to know him as our Father. That's why Christ taught us to pray, "Our Father who art in heaven, give us this day our daily bread."

A worried young man said to his friend, "I've looked to the right and to the left, and now I do not know where to turn. The friend replied, "Why don't you look up?" Look up and see your Father smiling on you. His smile has come upon the world in a strange and remarkable way. Look up and see three crosses raised against the sky. On the central cross, the Son of God died for the sins of the world. In him there is forgiveness and life. Look on his cross and accept his forgiveness as your own. Follow him where he leads, and know what it means to belong again to God's family.

God takes care of his family. No problems, no needs, no worries are too big or too little for him to take into his own heart. St. Paul said it this way: "He who did not spare his own Son but gave him up for us all, will he not also give us all things with him?" (Rom. 8:32, RSV).

By faith in Christ, God's Son, know in all truth that God is your Father. His name will be holy in the world. His kingdom will come, and his will shall be done. Pray, then, in all confidence, not hesitantly or doubtfully: "Our Father who art in heaven, give us this day our daily bread."

Our Lord's Prayer is not an invitation to laziness. Far from it. It is a prayer for God to give what we cannot get without him, without his gifts of time, health, brain, muscle, sun, rain, or the opportunity to work. Pray him to give, and he gives.

Why pray when God gives even without our asking? He makes his sun to rise on the evil and on the good, doesn't he? And sends rain on the just and on the unjust? Yes, he does. Yet, people go their way like pigs, filling their bellies at the trough of God's goodness and going away without thanksgiving. If you want to be a pig, go ahead! If you want to be human, pray, "Give us this day our daily bread."

When you receive God's gifts, credit the giver. The giver is good. You can depend on him. That is why we are to ask for *today* alone: "Give us *this day* our daily bread." Give us tomorrow the bread for tomorrow. Tomorrow is God's. It belongs to him. Putting your faith in Christ, you can say this quite naturally and mean it! Remember, it was Christ who said, "Do not be anxious, saying, 'What shall we eat, or what shall we drink, or what shall we wear?' For the Gentiles seek all these things; and your heavenly Father knows that you need them all. But seek first his kingdom and his righteousness and all these things shall be yours as well" (Matt. 6:31–33, RSV). Know it to be true, for God is Father and Christ is savior!

We pray not for ourselves alone: "Give *us* this day *our* daily bread." In praying for bread, we pray for the whole family, the whole human family. We ask God to take care of our needs and of the needs of others wherever they are. Praying, we share our needs with the rest of the world, and we promise to share what we have to fill that need in the rest of the world. We are concerned not merely with religious issues, but with everything else that troubles the human family. As Edna St. Vincent Millay put it in one of her poems, "For us Christians tragedy is only a Christ-distance away." We pray that way or we do not pray at all: "Father, give us this day our daily bread."

A couple of hundred years ago, it was considered blasphemous to recite the Lord's Prayer backward. It is just as blasphemous to turn the Lord's Prayer around today: to put ourselves first and God last, to accept the gift and forget the giver. Remembering the giver, and accepting his gifts with thanksgiving, we pray in the name of our Lord Jesus Christ: "Our Father who art in heaven, give us this day our daily bread."

The Disciples Asked the Lord: "Teach Us How to Pray."
The Lord Said, "Pray in This Way: 'Give Us This Day Our Daily Bread'"

Our Father in heaven, you know how we have to live with all the things that are needed for everyday life. Take care of all that, we pray, as only you can.

You clothe the lilies of the field, and your Son has promised that you will take care of those who have faith in you. We put ourselves into your hands and ask you to take care of us from day to day.

Make us thankful for ordinary things and not just the extraordinary ones—for the cut that healed quite naturally; for the hurt that has healed with time; for the last paycheck, for health to work every day; for children who obey most of the time; for parents who understand most of the time; for government officials with a conscience and also a heart, recognizing their responsibility to you; for food on the table, and for people who produce it; for kind friends and loving families; and also for grace in keeping kindness and love from being in short supply.

Give us the bread of life, along with the ordinary bread of today, in the name of your Son Jesus Christ.

Amen.

7. Forgive Us Our Trespasses

"Our Father who art in heaven, forgive us our sins as we forgive those who sin against us."

To forgive, we must forget. However, two things dare not be forgotten: (1) God forgives us before we can even think of forgiving others, and (2) forgiveness is the heartbeat of God in us. If we forget this, we shall never be able to forgive and forget. That is why the Lord bids us to pray, "Our Father who art in heaven, forgive us our debts (sins, trespasses) as we forgive our debtors (those who sin, trespass, against us)."

"Forgive us our sins." First things first. God forgives before we can forgive. We need forgiveness, you and I. We need forgiveness from God. We pray to God that he will forgive us.

We do not pray because God is unwilling to forgive. He is ready and willing to forgive. He has given his Son in our behalf, and he does forgive. We pray as debtors to whom God forgives everything. He is a giving and forgiving Father. St. James describes him as the "Giver God." So he is.

God is not the problem. We are. Here is something

most of us do not like to admit. We are debtors to the goodness and grace of God. Our debt is not just one solitary failure. We have debts, many of them. We feel the weight of our debts only when we put them on the scale of God's grace and goodness toward us.

Note that little word *and*. "*And* forgive us our debts." It reminds us of something that went before: "Give us this day our daily bread *and* forgive us our debts." Daily bread and forgiveness just about make up the total needs of humanity. God gives both. He gives us everything we need to support this body and life, not always as much as we think we could use but always as much as he knows we need. He gives us everything else we need along with daily bread. He forgives our debts, great as they are.

That is why we call him our Father. For us he gave his Son, whom he loves most dearly. For us the Son gave his holy life, paying the price of our sins. For us God did and does all this, out of his great love, so great that it is hard to understand. No wonder that men of old, astonished at the works of God, worshipped him: "Bless the Lord, O my soul, and forget not all his benefits; who forgiveth all thine iniquities, who healeth all thy diseases, who redeemeth thy life from destruction, who crowneth thee with loving kindness and tender mercy, who satisfieth thy mouth with good things" (Psalm 103:2–5, KJV). No wonder that Paul, marveling at the whole transaction of Christ's cross, exclaimed, "He that spared not his own Son, but delivered him up for us all, how shall he not with him also freely give us all things?" (Rom. 8:32, KJV).

The grace and goodness of God put us in his debt, one we can never repay: "If thou shouldest mark iniquities, O Lord, who shall stand?" (Psalm 130:4, KJV). None of us is going to make up the debts we owe to God. In God's forgiveness, there is healing of mind, soul, and body. It really does something for us to pray for God's forgiveness and then to accept the forgiveness for which we pray. It does something that only God can do: it makes people as God intended them to be, strong again in that dependence on God without which no one can really be oneself.

We cannot repay our debts to God. There are some things, however, that we can do. We can respond to his goodness with gratitude and worship. We can put our trust in his promises. We can respond to his love by learning to love in return, showing love both to God and to other people with whom we live and work.

Still, we can never worship, trust, and love to such an extent that any of us can pay off our debts to God. We are yet in his debt, as John Donne, seventeenth-century English poet and clergyman, personally confessed in "A Hymn to God the Father," that well-known poem which is really a play on his own name:

> Wilt Thou forgive that sin where I begun,
> Which is my sin, though it were done before?
> Wilt Thou forgive that sin, through which I run,
> And do run still: though still I do deplore?
> When Thou hast done, Thou hast not done,
> For I have more.
>
> Wilt Thou forgive that sin by which I have won
> Others to sin? and made my sin their door?
> Wilt Thou forgive that sin which I did shun
> A year, or two: But wallowed in, a score?
> When Thou hast done, Thou hast not done,
> For I have more.
>
> I have a sin of fear that, when I have spun
> My last thread, I shall perish on the shore;
> Swear by Thyself that at my death Thy Son
> Shall shine as He shines now, and heretofore:
> And, having done that, Thou has done.
> I fear no more.

For the sins we commit, for the sin of causing others to sin, and, last of all, for that characteristic human sin of fear, which is really lack of trust in God, we pray, "Our Father who art in heaven, forgive us our debts." This is the shoe that fits us all. When we pray that little word *forgive*, we must not forget for what we pray: "Our debts . . . send them away, send them away, send them away."

Praying *forgive*, we acknowledge that God does

forgive. He is the source of every good and perfect gift. He does send our sins away. He does charge our debts to someone else: His own unique and eternal Son, Jesus Christ, on whom our debts were piled. "He made him who knew no sin at all to be sin for us that we might be made the righteousness of God in him" (2 Cor. 5:21). We do have "redemption through his blood, even the forgiveness of sins" (Col. 1:14, KJV).

As the vacationers neared their summer home, they stopped for food. At the same time, they bought one of those "three-cornered strainers" for the kitchen sink. By mid-morning it was full, so they went out and bought a more adequate container—a step-on can. That, too, was filled by the following morning. Now the problem was getting to be basic. Thereupon, they drove the station wagon down to the hardware store and purchased a big galvanized can—in fact, they bought two. That solved the problem for a week. At the end of that time, there the problem was again.

Something had to be done. They decided to arrange for an outside agency to take it off their hands. And finally they got rid of the garbage.

This is a modern parable of what God wants each of us to do, day by day. He says, pray to the one who can take the garbage of life off our hands: "Our Father who art in heaven, forgive us our debts."

In biblical times, people were not generally brainwashed by subtle slogans to buy things for which they could not pay. As a result, there was no plan by which one's debts could be lumped into one big load to be repaid monthly out of one's regular salary. When someone incurred a debt he or she could not pay, he or she was often required to pledge another member of the family whose service constituted a guarantee against that debt. The prophet Nehemiah mentioned some people of his time who were so heavily mortgaged they had to give away their sons and daughters as surety for their debts (Neh. 5:2–3).

The great God gave away his Son for our debts. He came not to be served but to serve and to give his life as a ransom for the world. He died to take away the debts we could never repay. He rose again from the dead to assure everyone that his debts really have been paid. Because of the Son, there can be peace and prayer between us and our father. Knowing all this, the Son himself gave us this prayer that we might pray: "Father, forgive us our debts."

We have a covenant with God that he will forgive our debts. God's Son is the surety, the guarantee that God means business. He has already forgiven. You need not push him around, getting him to agree to forgive a few debts. We make his forgiveness our own when we pray, "Forgive us our debts."

Anyone living without the heavenly Father's forgiveness is like someone sleeping in a house that is on fire. Why live that way? Pray in all confidence, "Father, forgive us our debts." Pray in the spirit of Robert Southey, a poet laureate of England:

> Lord, who art merciful as well as just,
> Incline Thine ear to me, a child of dust,
> Not what I would do, O Lord, I offer Thee,
> Alas, but what I can.
> Father Almighty, who has made me man,
> And bade me look to heav'n, for Thou art there,
> Accept my sacrifice and humble prayer:
> Four things, which are in Thy treasury,
> I lay before Thee, Lord, with this petition:
> My nothingness, my wants, my sin, and my contrition.

Forget all that practical irreligion that may have prevented you from praying with a full heart, "Forgive us our debts." Forget all that pagan orthodoxy that cuts off people today from the roots of faith. Receive the good news of forgiveness as the exciting thing it really is. Every person can see that if God really is—and really forgives—this is wonderful news. We are not alone. Earth is not the whole story. The great God really cares. Because he cares, he shares. He forgives.

"Forgive us our debts." This comes first. Don't ever forget it! "Forgive us our debts as we forgive our debtors." Forgiveness is the heartbeat of God within our hearts. This is not just a practical gimmick to influence people or to make them feel good. It is an indispensable necessity.

After giving this whole prayer, our Lord took time to reemphasize this one fact: "For if you forgive men their trespasses, your heavenly Father also will forgive you; but if you do not forgive men their trespasses, neither will your Father forgive your trespasses" (Matt. 6:14–15, RSV).

People who refuse to forgive break the bridge over which they themselves must pass. Forgiveness is a dynamic force coming from the heart of God. It dare not be stopped by narrow-minded and indebted people. Peter once came to Jesus and asked, "Lord, how oft shall my brother sin against me, and I forgive him? till seven times?" Jesus answered, "I say not unto thee, until seven times: but, Until seventy times seven" (Matt. 18:21–22, KJV).

Then our Lord told the story about a king who was checking up on his servants. He noticed that one owed him 10,000 talents and gave the order that this man was to be sold, together with his family, and all he had was to be used for payment of the debt. The servant came to the king, pleading for patience and promising once again to pay the debt. The king, moved with compassion, let him go and forgave the debt. That same servant met a fellow servant out on the street who owed him a little debt, took him by the throat, and said, "Pay what you owe me." When this man was unable to pay, the forgiven but unforgiving servant had him thrown into prison. Someone told the king about it, and he called in the unforgiving man. This is what he said: "I forgave you all that debt; . . . and should not you have had mercy on your fellow servant, as I had mercy on you?" (Matt. 18:32–33, RSV). The last we hear of that man is not pleasant to recount. Our Lord added, "So also my heavenly Father will do to every one of you, if you do not forgive your brother from your heart" (Matt. 18:35, RSV).

This is no game God is playing. Nor can we play games when we pray, "Forgive us our debts as we forgive our debtors." It is not for us to say to God, "I'll forgive a few debts; now it's your turn." Forgiveness is not an isolated act but a pervading spirit, a spirit of compassion toward other people like ourselves, who need to have their debts forgiven.

Notice what the prayer says, "As we forgive our *debtors*." To forgive the debts is not enough. God forgives the debtors, not just the debts. He calls on every one of us to forgive in the same way, because all are indebted one to another.

No man is an island, living to himself alone. When you buy a loaf of bread, you are indebted not only to the storekeeper, but also to the baker, the miller, the farmer, and ultimately to God himself. We are in a constant chain of debt to our fellows, and they to us.

When we forgive, we set aside all debts, all transgressions, past, present, and future. When we forgive, we welcome our fellows into fellowship with us and with our heavenly Father. St. Paul put it all together in one short statement: "Be kind one to another, tenderhearted, forgiving one another, even as God for Christ's sake hath forgiven you" (Eph. 4:32, KJV).

Let us be clear about one thing: the fact that we forgive is not the reason God forgives us. Forgiveness begins with God. Forgiveness comes from God. Nothing in us, not even our willingness to forgive others, is sufficient reason for God to forgive us. He forgives freely without any merit or worthiness in us. When we refuse to forgive others, we demonstrate that repentance and love toward God run pretty shallow in our own lives.

Forgiveness comes quite naturally to God. We have to *learn* how to forgive. We have to learn how to forgive in the ordinary, everyday affairs of life. Learning that, we begin to understand how forgiveness becomes the heartbeat of God within our hearts.

Our natural tendency is not to forgive guilt but to avenge it. When somebody hurts us, our first thoughts are usually to pay back in kind. Some people carry these thoughts around with them for years, looking for a chance to get back at someone who has injured them. Christ tells us to forget those first thoughts, and also the long thoughts. He instructs us to pray, "Forgive us our debts as we forgive our debtors."

In the original language, the prayer is even stronger: "Forgive us our debts as *also* we forgive our debtors." Apparently, our Lord took it for granted that forgiveness is an ongoing process among people who are his followers. When we learn to forgive, that is a sign we have passed the test of discipleship. He has forgiven us, and we are members of his family. A wedding ring is a sign of wedded love and faithfulness; the forgiveness one extends to others is a sign that God's love and faithfulness has put a ring on one's finger.

Martin Luther wrote in his catechism, "If you therefore do not forgive, then do not think God forgives you. But if you forgive, you have this consolation and assurance, that you are forgiven in heaven. Not on account of your forgiving—for God forgives freely and without condition, out of pure grace, because he has promised, as the gospel teaches—but in order that he may set this up for our confirmation and assurance, for a sign alongside of the promise which accords with this prayer" (*Large Catechism*). This is exactly what our Lord meant when he said, "Forgive and you shall be fogiven."

It is not easy to forgive. Guilt makes us all angry. God's forgiveness, freely given and freely accepted, does away with that hostility toward God that the scriptures always associate with our sinful humanity. God's forgiveness builds a new gentleness, love, and understanding. Forgiveness makes gentle people. It turns us all into God's people.

Forgiveness from God is an upsetting thing: it turns people inside out and upside down. It goes all the way. Forgiveness never permits anyone to bury the hatchet while leaving the handle sticking out of the ground. Forgiveness finally buries the hatchet. It is the kind of thing that made Stephen pray when he was being stoned to death, "Lord, lay not this sin to their charge" (Acts 7:60, KJV).

"Father, forgive us our debts," past, present, and future. Forgive us for failing to make forgiveness genuine and warm. Forgive us for failing to remember that we have been forgiven. Help us to acknowledge our debts, because "if we say we have no sin, we deceive ourselves and the truth is not in us" (1 John 1:8, RSV). Help us to confess our sins, always remembering that we have a God who is faithful and just to forgive us our sins and to cleanse us from all our unrighteousness. Help us, O God, to forgive others as you have forgiven us. "Father, forgive us our sins as also we forgive those who sin against us."

The Disciples Asked the Lord: "Teach Us How to Pray."
The Lord Said, "Pray in This Way: 'Forgive Us Our Tres-
passes as We Forgive Those Who Trespass Against Us'"

Our Father in heaven, you are the Lord God Almighty.
Forgive us our trespasses against you and others, our debts
toward you and others.

Forgive us our ignorance, which makes us argue about
little things and forget the big things. We have sinned, we
have trespassed, we have become indebted to you, Father
in heaven, and we need your forgiveness.

For the sake of your Son Jesus, forgive us what we have
done wrong and failed to do right. We confess that we are
not all that we should be, or all that we are reputed to be.
We are human, and in that very humanity of ours we need
your forgiveness.

Give us grace, our Father in heaven, to forgive others.
Give us the grace that knowing ourselves forgiven, really
forgiven, we may be able to overcome our grudges and be
willing to forgive.

When you forgive, Father, you forget. You just put our
sins out of your sight. Help us to forgive one another in
the same way.

We ask this in Jesus' name.
Amen.

8. Lead Us Not into Temptation, But Deliver Us from Evil

"Our Father who art in heaven, lead us not into temptation but deliver us from evil."

A well-known German theologian, Helmut Thielicke, has described the modern human as a poker player, ready to take the risks of climbing to bold heights or of descending to the lowest depths. People call this "living it up" or "living dangerously."

By contrast, the person who prays, "Our Father who art in heaven, lead us not into temptation but deliver us from evil," sounds as if he or she were playing it safe. Almost by definition, this is old-fashioned. Even worse, to many it appears a ludicrous attempt to escape reality: one is bound to get into trouble, they say, and it must be our business to *get ourselves out* of trouble once we have gotten ourselves in.

People who understand this petition of our Lord's Prayer as an attempt to escape from life or to evade reality do not understand it at all. This is not the prayer of a weakling. It represents a healthy respect for the pitfalls of life and a wholesome regard for the power and grace of God to help us make our way through life, battling our own weaknesses and the hostility of other people.

The New English Bible translates this two-part petition thus: "Do not bring us to the test, but save us from the evil one."

God is not the enemy. He is not forever trying to trick people into making a misstep. Let that be understood right at the outset.

But God does provide tests, even for the hardiest of souls. With his own tests, which are never too hard to bear when we meet them with faith and fortitude, God leads weaklings to strength and leads the strong to heights they would otherwise never be able to reach.

What is it then for which we pray in this petition? We pray not to be drawn into temptation of our own accord, apart from the will of God. "Watch and pray," our Lord urged his disciples, "that ye enter not into temptation" (Matt. 26:41, KJV).

St. James made it quite clear that when someone yields to temptation it is not God's fault. People yield to temptation because they want to yield. They like to skirt the edges of evil and then slip in. We pray in this petition that we may not fall into temptation. There is a good deal of difference between falling into temptation and meeting temptation with faith and courage.

In this petition, we pray that God would not let us alone but that he would guard and protect us from the real enemy—the evil that is in the world, the evil one who would like to trick every one of us so that we fall into temptation.

This is Christ's prayer. It is intended for people who know Christ and trust in him. Indeed, the prayer itself is an inducement to know Christ and to trust in him: "Our Father who art in heaven, lead us not into temptation but deliver us from evil." Of this prayer, Martin Luther once said, "Even though we be godly now and stand before God with a good conscience, we must pray that He would not suffer us to relapse and yield to trials and temptations."

All of us know what a relapse does to someone who has been ill. It is a definite setback, which could be more dangerous than the original illness.

A relapse in morality or in lifestyle can mean a departure from the faith of Christ that has brought someone out of the morass into which that person originally fell. That relapse can be fatal, as many people have found out who have toyed with their faith and flirted with temptation. That is why our Lord urges us to pray, fervently and with a full heart, "Our Father who art in heaven, bring us not to the test that overtakes us unawares or finds us falling in of our own volition, but deliver us from that evil that is always trying to overtake and to overcome us."

It is popular today to think of sin as old-fashioned and of temptation as something to be met by yielding to it rather than by overcoming it. Talk of sin is looked on as unhealthy and unwholesome because it gives a person an unnecessary sense of guilt. American psychologist Karl Menninger wrote a book about this entitled *Whatever Became of Sin?* People who have tried this lackadaisical view of sin can tell you how it works out. It results in nagging feelings of guilt that cannot be ignored, for the simple reason that conscience will not let one rest. People who try to minimize sin can tell you how it takes over and damages lives; it results in broken marriages, ruined careers, loss of friendship, disrespect of children for their parents, and bitterness that can last a lifetime.

Still, some people will not listen. They know that one misstatement by a politician can lose the election. But *their* own mistakes, no matter how ghastly, seem to be of little importance. Somehow, they assume that others must ignore or disrespect their actions. These people expect God, against whose holiness and justice their offenses have been committed, to ignore their sins as well! Talk about running away from reality! This is it!

It has often been said that in warfare the first principle is to recognize and to respect the capabilities of your opponent. This is to face reality, the first step on the road to victory. The next step is to draw on all your own resources, and those of your allies, for the struggle ahead. This prayer looks to the resources of our one great ally in the struggle against evil. Recognizing what we are up against, we pray, "Our Father who art in heaven, lead us not into temptation, but deliver us from evil."

We pray for deliverance from evil and from the evil one. The devil is our enemy. His allies are all those influences that would drag us away from God. The world has a marvelous ally in our own flesh: that disposition in each of us to go our own way instead of God's way. Don't pretend that these forces do not exist. Don't look the other way; they are right at your door. If you are a normal human being, you know exactly what I am talking about. You know what it means to feel guilty. You can't get rid of that feeling just by burying it deep down inside. It has to be faced. Facing it, we pray, "Our Father who art in heaven, lead us not into temptation but deliver us from evil."

This prayer is not just a good-luck charm. Directed to our Father in heaven, it means exactly what it says. It takes for granted that there is a loving Father who hears our prayer and can do something about it. He can help, and he will help. He does care, and he will take a hand in the ordinary affairs of our lives. The onslaught of evil, or even the invitation to evil, can be the occasion for the exercise of his power. It is for this we pray when we say, "Our Father who art in heaven, lead us not into temptation but deliver us from evil."

Our Father, to whom we pray, does care. He has proved that once and for all in his Son, Jesus Christ, who dared every danger in behalf of each one of us individually and of all of us together. He was tempted, even as we are, but remained without sin. Having lived his life in complete obedience to his Father's will, he gave that innocent life for all of us, paying the price we would otherwise have had to pay ourselves. In his death on the Cross there is life for everyone. In his atonement, there is forgiveness for everyone. In his resurrection from the dead, there is strength for everyone to meet temptation and overcome it. In Christ, there is power to go on to higher things.

This is true. Christ came to be your savior and mine. Because of him, we have reason to hope, you and I, and to pray, "Our Father who art in heaven, lead us not into temptation, but deliver us from evil."

On some mountain roads, you can see signs saying, "Watch for falling rocks." Most of us drive blithely on as if the signs mean nothing at all—until we meet a big pile of rocks just fallen from the hillside before we arrived. We are reminded that it could have fallen on *us*.

St. Paul wrote to a young man, with every bit of

realism at his command, "And the Lord shall deliver me from every evil work, and will preserve me unto his heavenly kingdom, to whom be glory forever and ever. Amen" (2 Tim. 4:18, KJV).

Where did Paul get his confidence? Again and again he tells us. Having faith in Christ and knowing why he died and why he rose again from the dead, St. Paul recognized himself as a forgiven child of God. That was enough to give him courage. From then on he addressed God as *Father*. I have no doubt that St. Paul prayed every day, "Our Father who art in heaven, lead us not into temptation but deliver us from evil."

St. Paul tells us, "I can do all things through Christ which strengtheneth me" (Phil. 4:13, KJV). God himself will not introduce you to any temptation that you are not capable of handling. He knows what you can take, and he will not hand you more than you can bear. If you are talked into temptation, it will be only because you yourself wanted to be tempted. To counteract that inclination, every one of us must draw on the power of our heavenly Father. We pray, "Lead us not into temptation, but deliver us from evil."

Our heavenly Father helps us over the difficulties of life. He knows how to use temptation even for his good purpose. Testing, trial, and temptation are never easy to take, but every test, every trial, every temptation becomes an asset instead of a liability when it is overcome under the guidance of our watchful and loving heavenly Father.

Because of the St. Lawrence Seaway, ships sail inland from the Atlantic Ocean to Lake Superior, rising to an elevation of over 600 feet in the course of their voyage. The elevation is accomplished by a series of locks. After the ship enters a lock, the lock is flooded with water so that the boat rises to the level of the canal beyond the lock and can sail on at the higher altitude toward the destination far inland.

So God, through the tests he provides, leads us on from where we are to where he is—always drawing us closer to himself. We pray in this petition that we may not run aground through our own willfulness or waywardness and spoil all our Father's good plans for us. We pray for his kind leading: "Our Father who art in heaven, lead us not into temptation, but deliver us from evil."

We are not perfect, and we will not be perfect this side of heaven. We can fall into temptation. Even the most respected of us can suffer relapse from the high ground to which we have been called by faith in Christ. So we admit the gravity of life and our need of God's help all along the way. We willingly pray, "Our Father who art in heaven, lead us not into temptation but deliver us from evil."

Praying, we are only being honest with ourselves

and honest to our God. In Buffalo, New York, a young man was given a lobster dinner and a $100 reward for returning to a bank a satchel he had found containing $5,000. The young man had not told anyone about his action. When asked why, he replied, "I didn't want to be called a fool for returning the money." Today when people are readily called fools for practicing the ordinary virtue of honesty, don't be ashamed of such a life for yourself. Be honest with yourself and honest toward God. Pray daily as our Lord taught us, "Our Father who art in heaven, lead us not into temptation but deliver us from evil."

The Disciples Asked the Lord: "Teach Us How to Pray." The Lord Said, "Pray in This Way: 'Lead Us Not into Temptation, But Deliver Us from Evil'"

Our Father in heaven, we pray that you will keep your promise not to allow such temptation to come on us as we cannot endure. You promised that no temptation of your children would be unendurable, and we hold you to that promise.

Give us newness of life by your great resurrection power, that we may face temptation and even go out to meet temptation without the lust of the flesh and the lust of the eye and the pride of life that always cause our downfall. Humble us under your mighty hand, Father, that we may stand tall in your grace and glory, as did your Son Jesus.

By your grace, deliver us from the power of evil and Satan. You have the power to deliver even as you delivered your Son Jesus from the chains of death. Deliver by that power of yours, and give us strength to walk in newness of life.

As you set free the captives and give sight to those who cannot see, give us the deliverance and freedom to serve you and others in our lives with joyful hearts, full of faith and love that are in your Son, Christ Jesus.

Amen.

9. Thine Is the Kingdom

"Our Father who art in heaven, . . . thine is the kingdom, and the power, and the glory, for ever. Amen."

Our Lord gave us his prayer in order to teach us how to pray. We pray for ourselves and for others who need him. When we talk to him, it is never just "my Father" but "our Father."

When we say from the heart, "our Father," we recognize that we really are his children, not just because we say we are but because we really are. "Our Father" is not just a lovely expression, but a statement of fact based on hard reality: the cross of our Father's Son, Jesus Christ. God is our Father in Christ, the Father's Son. Christ came to be God's man. As God's man, he died in our behalf. As God's man, he was raised from the dead by the glory of his Father to be the living Lord of heaven and earth. Now it is true, as St. Paul said, "We are all the sons and daughters of God by faith in Jesus Christ" (Gal. 3:26).

When we say, "our Father," we recognize that we are not the only ones to have been redeemed by the life, death, and resurrection of Jesus Christ. There are others, many others. When he died, all died. He died for all that they who live should not henceforth live for themselves but for him who died for them and rose again. In Christ, God reconciled the whole world unto himself, not counting our sins against us. This is the way it is: he is the lamb of God who takes away the sins of the *world*. We have company, a lot of company.

No one is excluded from the privilege of calling God "Father." No one stands outside the redeeming love of his heavenly Father, expressed so graphically and so brutally on the cross of Calvary where the Son of God died for the sins of the whole world.

When we say "our Father," we identify ourselves with the whole church throughout the world, the redeemed of God and all the faithful who trust in Christ as savior. With all of them, we share God's forgiveness of sins, joy, hope, peace, life, and eternal salvation.

Finally, we identify ourselves with God himself when we say to him: "You are our Father." We praise him with this prayer: "Thine is the kingdom, and the power, and the glory for ever. Amen." To him our prayer is directed, and on him it depends. The focus of our attention at the beginning of this prayer was on him, "Our Father, . . . Hallowed be thy name, thy kingdom come. Thy will be done on earth as it is in heaven." At the end of our praying, we remember him, only him! "For thine is the kingdom, and the power, and the glory, for ever. Amen."

We give him the kingdom, the power, and the glory—recognizing his right to have and to hold and to share as he wills—when we pray for ourselves and for others in this prayer our Lord taught us to pray. We pray for ourselves and for all people when we say, "Give us and forgive us; lead us not into temptation but deliver us. Thine is the kingdom, and the power, and the glory."

When you pray for someone else, you may find it healthy to put his or her name right into this prayer: "Our Father who art in heaven, thy name be hallowed in my friend Janet (or my sister, or my brother). Thy kingdom come in her, thy will be done in her today as it is in heaven. Give Janet today her daily bread; forgive Janet her trespasses, and help her to forgive all who trespass against her; let her not succumb today to temptation, but deliver her even now from all evil." Learn to pray by praying for others. You can do this quite simply: "Our Father, look upon your daughter Janet, feed her, forgive her, lead her, and be a Father to her this day, for yours is the kingdom, the power, and the glory forever and ever. Amen."

You can put many people into your prayers: your father and mother; your wife or your husband; your children; your friends; your neighbors; your pastor and the teachers of your church; the mayor, councilors, and the judges of your town or city; the governing authorities; anyone who is in need or in trouble; the sick; the lonely; people who do not know where to turn; those who are suffering from slander or from what they have done to hurt their own reputations; all who need God's help in whatever way. Pray for them by name.

Do you believe that the kingdom, the power, and the glory belong to him? Pray then for those masses of people throughout the world who are looking for a way out, for the sophisticated who do not know God, for the college students who want to know him, for company executives and union leaders, for city dwellers and for country people. Pray for the spiritually ignorant and the spiritually comfortable, the cynics and the doubters, the secularists and the materialists. Pray for them because you really believe that the kingdom, the power, and the glory belong to your heavenly Father. You know your Father cares and you are convinced that he can take care of those in need. Your heavenly Father really has the kingdom, the power, and the glory, and your prayers are worth the time and effort!

This doxology is scriptural, although it was probably not a part of the prayer as first given by our Lord. It is a response of believing hearts, coming down to us from most ancient times, summing up what the scriptures say about God, our Father.

Some Christian people do not use this doxology as part of the Lord's Prayer. Others use it only in their liturgical worship. It is worth saying just to remind ourselves to whom we pray, for what we pray, and through whom we pray. We pray in the name of Christ, who gave us this prayer; we pray for the things Christ told us to pray for; and we pray to the God whom Christ has instructed us to call "our Father." To him belong the kingdom, the power, and the glory, not only now but forever and ever. So be it!

When we say "Amen," we are saying, "This is really true," or "This is really the way it is!" Everything here counts. This is no idle gesture. This "Amen" echoes St. Paul: "This is a faithful saying and worthy of all acceptation, that Jesus Christ came into the world to save sinners" (1 Tim. 1:15, kjv). In saying "Amen" to Christ, we say "Amen" to the Father. He is our Father. He looks out for his children. He wants us to pray, and he hears our prayer. To that we say, "Amen. This is most certainly true!"

Here at the end, we turn from petition to gratitude. This is our response or "worship" for the goodness and the grace of God. What other response can we have? He promises his good gifts, forgiveness and life; we in turn trust him. He showers his love on us; we love him in return. When he gives, we are grateful.

We are grateful to God not just for what he gives but for what he is. I was told by a friend of mine, who is a fine Christian man today, that he had never prayed in his life until he was a student at a university in a European country. There one night he kneeled down in his room to pray for the first time in his life. All he could do was to thank God that he existed. It was not a meaningless gesture. His whole life was changed from that moment on. He thanked God for the mere fact that he was no longer alone in this great world. He knew that God was there, and later on he discovered that God is a rewarder of those who diligently seek him.

No one can talk you into the spirit or the attitude of prayer. You will have to find that out for yourself. You will find it when you are grateful. The bitter or the small spirit never finds God. Gratitude enlarges the heart and overcomes self-will. Gratitude recognizes God the giver, who cannot be pushed around, even by the prayers of his people. God, our Father, responds with grace and his good heart to the prayers of those who recognize themselves as needy, hungry, thirsty souls, unclothed until they are clothed with the garments of righteousness that God alone can give us.

The words of this closing became a part of the

Lord's Prayer throughout the Christian world during the days when the church was being persecuted from pillar to post. The more martyrs there were, the more widespread these words of praise became. This is what people say when they are in trouble, when they are sick or dying, when they are down and out. These words echo Stephen's when he was being stoned to death and saw heaven open up before him and Jesus standing at the right hand of God: "Thine is the kingdom, and the power, and the glory forever and ever. Amen."

Not so very long ago a man arose in central Europe and proclaimed that his kingdom or "Reich" would last a thousand years. Hitler did not hesitate to put his Reich in the place of the kingdom of God. That man is dead, and his kingdom is dead with him. But the kingdom of God stands out more glorious than ever before. It is true! The kingdom does belong to God!

Let's face it! Our world is impressed by power. Some people and nations will listen only to the voice of power. Even in democratic countries, the politician who wins an election is powerful, no matter how closely he or she squeaked by. Power is the thing, and whoever holds power commands allegiance.

Is there any power that can change our world and turn it upside down? That can change the hearts of people and turn them from thoughts of evil to thoughts of peace? Is there any power that can make us again as God intended us to be? Yes! This is what we are saying: to God belongs the power—the power to create and to destroy, the power to judge and the power to forgive, the power to hear the prayers of his people and the power to do what they ask. To him we say, "Thine is the kingdom, and the power. Amen."

The kingdoms of the world glory in their ability to lord it over one another. This seems to be our ultimate temptation: to boss our fellows. Even the littlest of us, no matter how small, long to lord it over someone else. Christ said to his followers: "It shall not be so among you. Whoever would be great among you will have to be servant of all" (Matt. 23:11). This great truth was put to work in his own character and mission. He came not to be served but to serve and to give his life a ransom for the world. A servant of servants, he washed the feet of his disciples. More than a gesture, his action was the ultimate example of his grace and generosity.

The glory of God expressed itself in a most remarkable way of giving. The Son of God came as a servant of servants, emptied himself of his glory, laid aside the privilege of his godhead (although he was always God), and laid down his life on a cross for the life of the world. Here is glory! Here is giving! This is the glory of which we speak when we say to our

Father: "Thine is the kingdom, and the power, and the glory forever and ever. Amen."

Here at the end of our Lord's Prayer, we dismiss every coldness and every lukewarmness, every doubt and every hesitation, every anxiety and every fear; here flood in all faith and all love, all fire and all warmth, all confidence and all courage. Here it is, summed up in one short, grand encomium to the most high. As his sons and daughters in Christ the savior, we call him our Father. "Our Father who art in heaven, thine is the kingdom, and the power, and the glory forever and ever. Amen!"

> Thine is the kingdom, unto thee
> Shall bow in homage ev'ry knee.
> And thine the pow'r; no pow'r shall be
> That is not overcome by thee.
> The glory thine; by ev'ry tongue
> Thy praise shall be forever sung.

> (MARTIN H. FRANZMANN,
> "O Thou, Who Hast of Thy Pure Grace")

The Disciples Asked the Lord: "Teach Us How to Pray." The Lord Said, "Pray in This Way: 'Thine Is the Kingdom and the Power and the Glory Forever and Ever. Amen'"

You rule, and you rule alone. We praise you for your Son, in whose hand you have placed the kingdom. We do not always act as if he is Lord and Lord alone. But now we praise you for your rule, and we pray that you will rule over us.

Yours is the glory, and yours alone. There is none like you in all the land, all the world, all the universe. There is none who even approaches your glory. And we do not even come close to the glory you expect of us. Thanks to you, Father in heaven, for your grace in showing forth your glory in the face of Jesus Christ, our mediator, our savior, our Lord.

Exercise your power in the world and also in our hearts, our Father in heaven. Send your Holy Spirit to empower our lives, giving us confidence in your forgiving heart, and putting steel in our backbones to stand up and be counted for you.

Yours is the kingdom, the power, and the glory, forever and ever.

Amen.

10. Amen

"Jesus said to him, 'Amen, amen, I say to you, you will see heaven opened, and the angels of God ascending and descending upon the Son of Man'" (John 1:51).

Everything belongs to God. It all comes from him. His is the kingdom, his is the power, his is the glory. It is all his as long as time shall last, and even beyond —forever.

It is what we say at the end of the Lord's Prayer: "Thine is the kingdom, and the power, and the glory, for ever." Now comes one more word, short, incisive, and to the point: "Amen."

It is our word to him. Even that comes from him. This is his word. The Lord used it often. He liked it. "Amen," he said, "the world will rejoice and you will be sorrowful, but your sorrow will be turned into joy" (John 16:20). In the last hours, on his cross, he turned to the crucified criminal by his side, and he said, "Amen, amen, I say to you, today you will be with me in paradise" (Luke 23:43).

It is his word, "Amen." He used it often. Right at the beginning, when he first met the men who would become his disciples, he said to one of them, "Amen, amen, I say to you, you will see heaven opened, and the angels of God ascending and descending upon the Son of Man" (John 1:51). The man to whom he said that was named Nathanael, at first glance a singularly unattractive character. He always said what he was thinking. Many people did not care to have him around. But the Lord picked him.

It was in Galilee. He found Philip and said to him, "Follow me." Now Philip was from Bethsaida, the city of Andrew and Peter. Philip found Nathanael, and said to him, "We have found him of whom Moses in the law and also the prophets wrote, Jesus of Nazareth, the son of Joseph." Nathanael said to him, "Can anything good come out of Nazareth?" Philip said to him, "Come and see." Jesus saw Nathanael coming to him and said of him, "Behold, an Israelite indeed, in whom there is no guile!" Nathanael said to him, "How do you know me?" Jesus answered him, "Before Philip called you, when you were under the fig tree, I saw you." Nathanael answered him, "Rabbi, you are the Son of God! You are the king of Israel!" Jesus answered him, "Because I said to you, 'I saw you under the fig tree,' do you believe? You shall see greater things than these." And Jesus said to him, "Amen, amen, I say to you, you shall see the heavens opened, and the angels of God ascending and descending upon the Son of Man" (John 1:45-51).

It is the first time, as far as I know, that Jesus is reported to have used the word "amen" in his public ministry. It was, as always, his last word, too. It was the take-off point for new things, with the solidity of truth behind, underneath, and around everything.

It is a great word. Today, in Papua, New Guinea, in the pidgin language, "Amen" is translated simply, "True." With that word, the people of New Guinea end the Lord's Prayer and all their prayers: "True." It is certainty, faith, and hope all wrapped into one word. It is assurance and commitment.

When Jesus used the word, "Amen," he put himself squarely behind everything he was saying. When we use it at the end of a prayer, we put ourselves squarely into the hands of the God to whom we pray. "Thine is the kingdom and the power and the glory, forever and ever. Amen." So we close our Lord's Prayer.

It is like saying to God, "I am with you. You can count on me. Now let's get on with it." It is the word of commitment with which people commit themselves every day in the most ordinary and also in the most sacred relationships. It is straightforward, direct, and honest. It is not tongue-in-cheek. It can't be said with a straight face when you mean something else. It is "Amen," and that means "Yes!"

Two friends of mine wrote a little song.* It starts out this way:

And God said Yes! Yes! Yes!
Said yes to the world once more,
Said yes with a cosmic roar, that opened that other door,
God said yes, man, yes.

At creation God said, Yes, let's splash the sky with light,
Let's float the earth in space, Let's dance away the night,
And God said yes, man, yes.

And God said, Yes, let Jesus Christ be born,
Let's find him in the straw, Let's blast the shepherd's horn
And God said yes, Son, yes.

And God said, yes, yes, to his broken Son,
Said yes to his open wound, yes to the broken tomb,
And God said yes, Son, yes.

And God said yes we will leap the swirling sky,
We will leap the hungry grave, we will never stop to die,
And God said yes, man, yes.

And God says yes to that other door,
God says yes when other men say no,

* Adapted from "Debbie's Song—And God Said, Yes!" from *For Mature Adults Only*, by Norman C. Habel and Richard Koehneke. Used by permission of Fortress Press.

Says yes with a cosmic roar
Says yes, man, with me.

That's God, and it's his son, Jesus Christ: Amen, Amen, yes, yes. "I say to you you will see the heavens opened and the angels of God ascending and descending upon the Son of Man" (John 1:51). Jesus is the one, for all people everywhere, the one of God's own choosing. He is the one mediator between his God and his children. He is God's yes to the world, a world that has learned mostly to say only no.

We use many words that are not English in origin. They have become a part of our language. Some of them are French, like *coup d'etat* or *cul-de-sac*. Others are German, like *Weltanschauung*. Still others are like *boondocks*, which I was told in the Philippines is the only word that has come into the English language from Tagalog, the official language of the Philippine Islands.

There are many words like that, and "Amen" is one of them. It is his word. His disciples reported it to us because he used it often. In Hebrew and Aramaic, it means "yes." We speak it at the end of a prayer as God speaks it to us at the beginning. It is his "Yes" to us in Jesus Christ. It is our "Yes" to him, also, in Jesus Christ.

God says, "You can take my word for it." Then he speaks his word. As St. Paul said, "All the promises of God are 'Amen' in Christ. All of the promises of God are 'Yes' in Him" (2 Cor. 1:20). They are certain, firm, and sure. At the end of the Bible, in the Revelation of St. John, Jesus himself is called the great "Amen." He is God's ultimate "Yes" to the world. He is its forgiveness and life.

For anything in your life that needs forgiveness, Jesus is your "Amen." He died for your sins. If there is any worry or anxiety about the future, Jesus is your "Amen." He was raised from the dead, and he lives for you. He is Lord. If there is anything at all that keeps you from opening up your life to God, Jesus is your "Amen." He can be trusted. He is Lord of your life. Because Jesus is our "Amen," we say so at the end of his prayer. He likes that word, and so do we. "Amen."

When we say "Amen," we claim Christ as our own. By his death on a cross, Jesus Christ claims you as his own. You can turn away from him, you can ignore him, you can reject him, but he is still the "Amen." He says to you right now, "There are better things to come. You will see greater things than a cross, or even a tomb from which the stone has been rolled away. You will see the angels of God ascending and descending on Christ. "Verily, verily," "Truly, truly," "Surely, surely," "Amen, amen!"

It's a great thing to know God in Jesus Christ. Many people claim to know him, but all they know is that God has the power to pass judgment on them. They have the idea that somehow they can satisfy that judgment by being good or trustworthy or respectable. That isn't enough, and it never will be. There is no way except by his grace to stand in the presence of God. Through his forgiveness, his gift of life, he commits to us his Son Jesus Christ as his ultimate "Amen!"

That's the beginning of great things in which people like us can have a part. "You will see," He says, "Amen and amen."

It happens to quite ordinary people. Philip had one distinction: he was an ordinary man from Bethsaida, the city of Andrew and Peter. There was nothing particularly outstanding about Philip. He was not picked because he was exceptional. But Jesus said to him, "Follow me" (John 1:43, RSV). Just as simple as that.

Philip found Nathanael and said to him with unaccustomed enthusiasm, "I have found him of whom Moses and the law and also the prophets wrote, Jesus of Nazareth, son of Joseph" (John 1:45). Nathanael replied with that sardonic humor that seems to have been characteristic of him, "Can anything good come out of Nazareth?" (John 1:46). Verily, verily, certainly, certainly, truly, truly, surely, surely, nothing good can come from a small town like that. "We don't need another prophet," said

Nathanael, "and we certainly don't need one from a place like Nazareth."

These men did not go around with holy looks making holy sounds. When they said, "Amen," it came out of their ordinary humanity, ennobled by the faith they had in Christ Jesus, the one mediator between God and people everywhere.

We can do today what Philip did for Nathanael. We can say to each other, "Come and see." Come and see Jesus Christ. Verily, verily, truly, truly, surely, surely, he is God's "Yes," his "Amen," to you!

All through their lives, Christ's disciples pointed to him. How great the Church would be throughout the world, if everywhere it pointed to Jesus Christ and only to him. He is the glory of the church. The invitation to come and see him has the power of God's Holy Spirit within it. When we come, you and I, we have to say, "Amen. Jesus has died and we are yours, God. In him, we are yours. Together with him, we are yours. Amen to you, Lord God, for yours is the kingdom and the power and the glory forever and ever."

Nathanael was having a siesta under a fig tree. He wasn't thinking religious thoughts, but the Lord found him right there, in the ordinary ways of human life. Nathanael was not going to be taken in by anybody. The Lord found him, and he found the

Lord, that day. It's as great and simple as that. He found the Lord that day. Amen, truly, verily, certainly, surely, he found the Lord that day!

There are better things than stewing underneath a fig tree. "Amen, Amen, you will see the angels of God ascending and descending upon the Son of Man." There are great things to come. It is the hazard of faith to follow him, but day by day the great God himself says "Yes" to that faith, and great things, sometimes unnoticed, begin to happen.

"Amen, and amen, I say to you! If you ask anything of the Father, he will give it to you in my name" (John 16:23). "Amen, Amen, I say to you, he who believes in me will also do the works that I do, and greater works than these will he do because I go to the Father" (John 14:12). "Amen, Amen, I say to you. The day will come when you will see the angels of God ascending and descending upon the Son of Man" (John 1:51). "Amen, Amen, I say to you. He who receives anyone whom I send, receives me and he who receives me, receives him who sent me" (John 13:20).

"Amen," my friends. It is his first and last word. If you have never said it before, say it now. "Amen." No matter how often you have said it, say it again with warm, generous assent to him: "Amen, Lord God, our Father. . . . Thine is the kingdom and the power and the glory forever and ever! Amen."